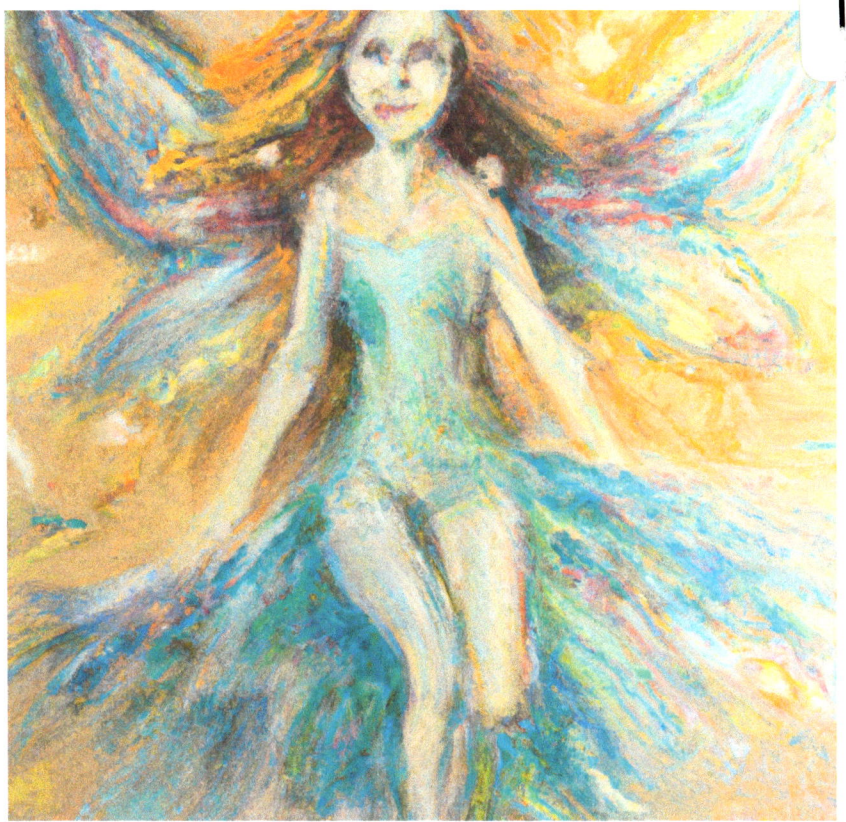

by Julie Ann Shaffer

This edition first published in 2023 by Julie Ann Shaffer.
Published by Shaffer Designs of Emerald, PA.
All rights reserved.
No part of this publication may be reproduced or distributed in any form
or by any means without the permission of the owner.
While we have made every effort to ensure the accuracy of the
information in this book, we cannot be held liable for any errors, omissions or inconsistencies.

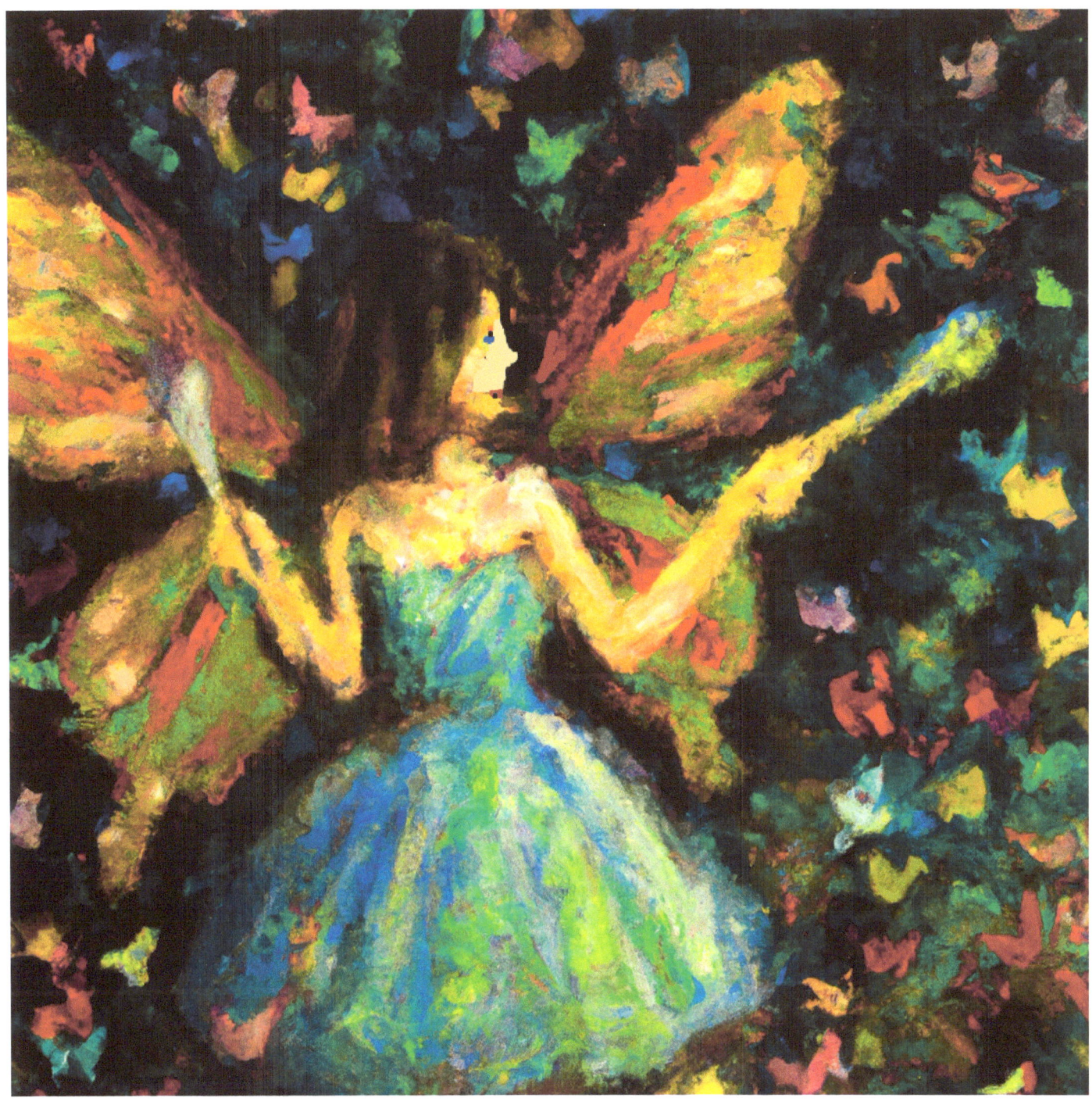

Impressionist Fairy Prints by Julie Ann Shaffer

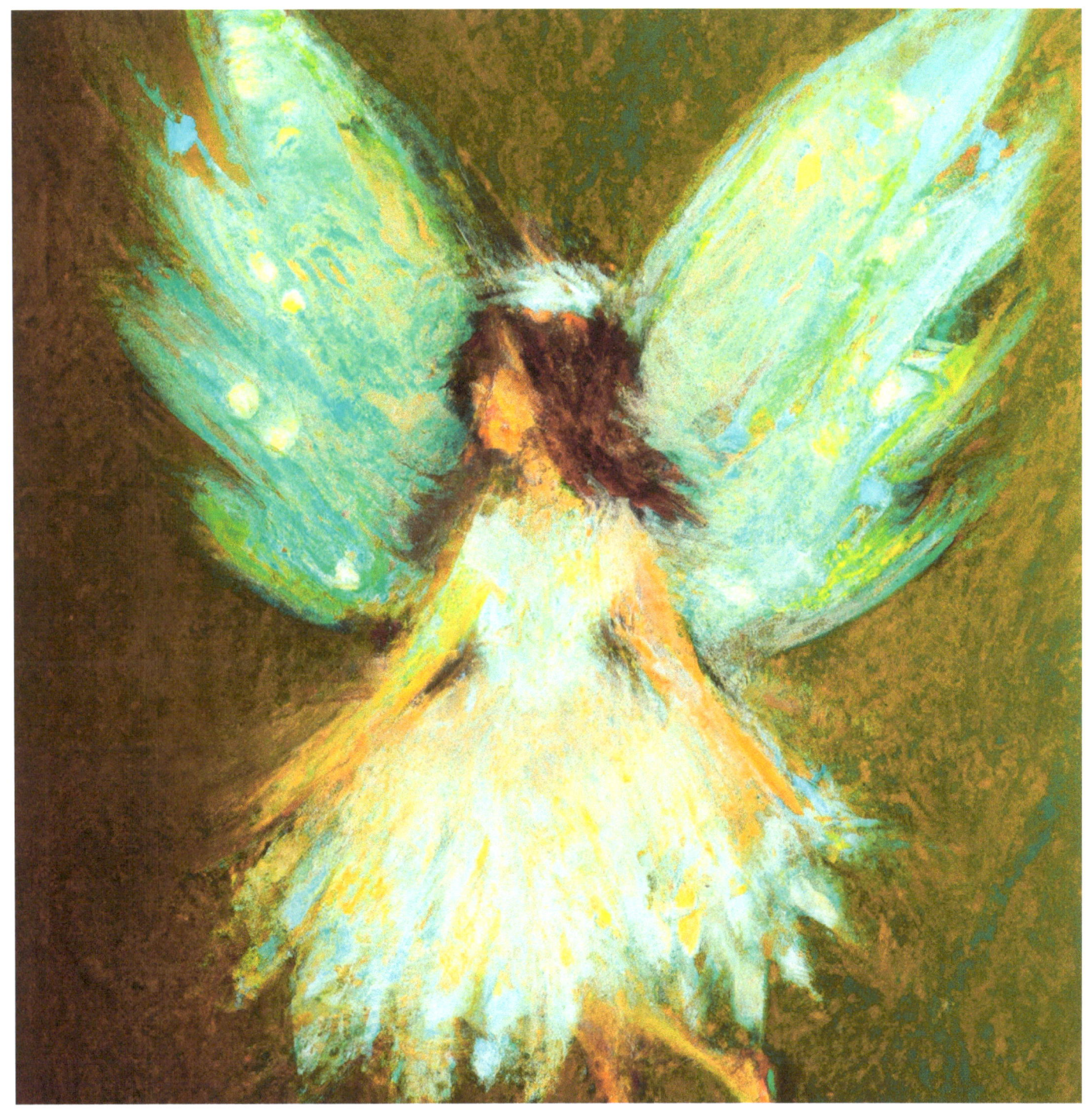

Impressionist Fairy Prints by Julie Ann Shaffer

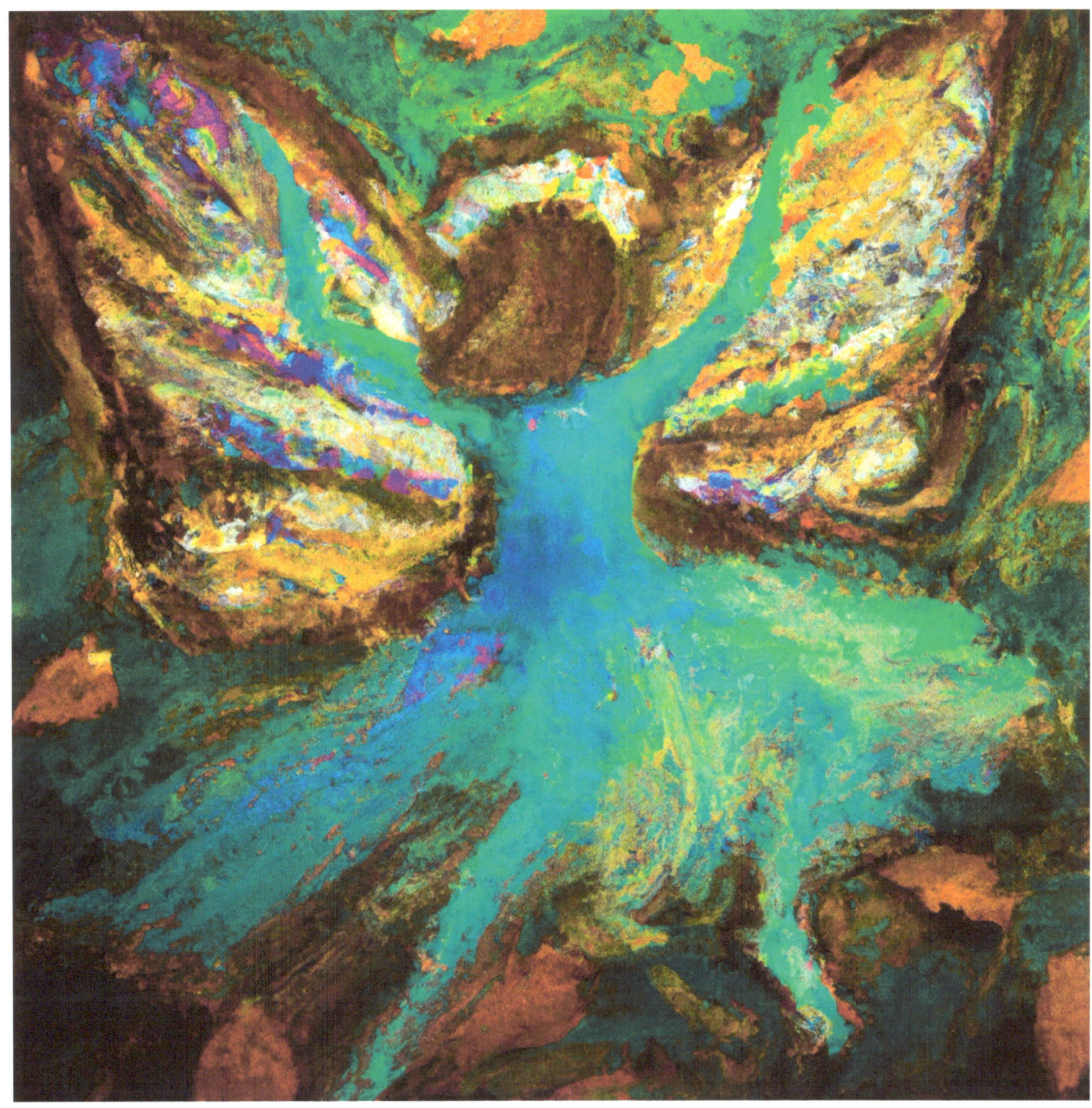

Impressionist Fairy Prints by Julie Ann Shaffer

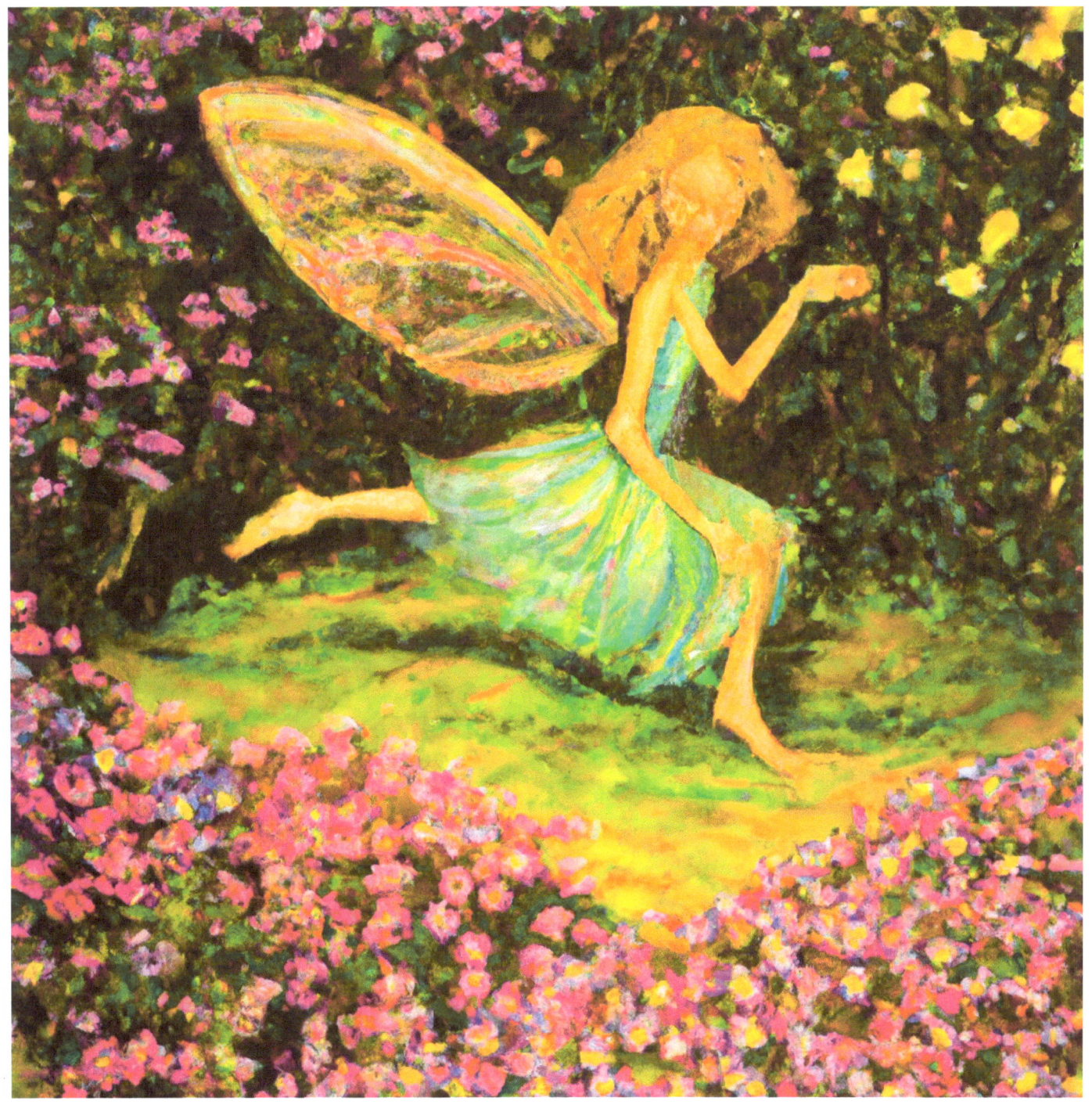

Impressionist Fairy Prints by Julie Ann Shaffer

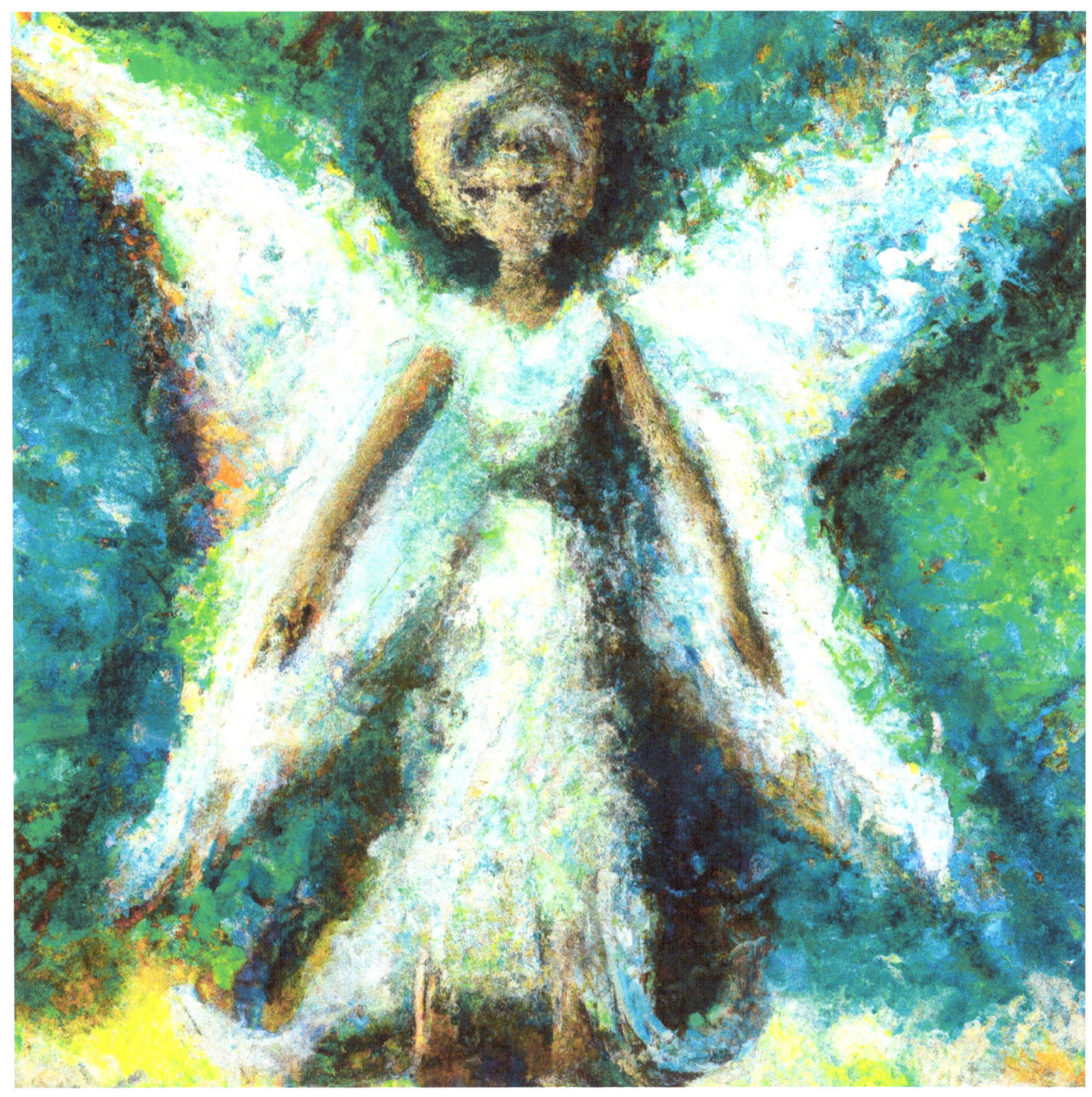

Impressionist Fairy Prints by Julie Ann Shaffer

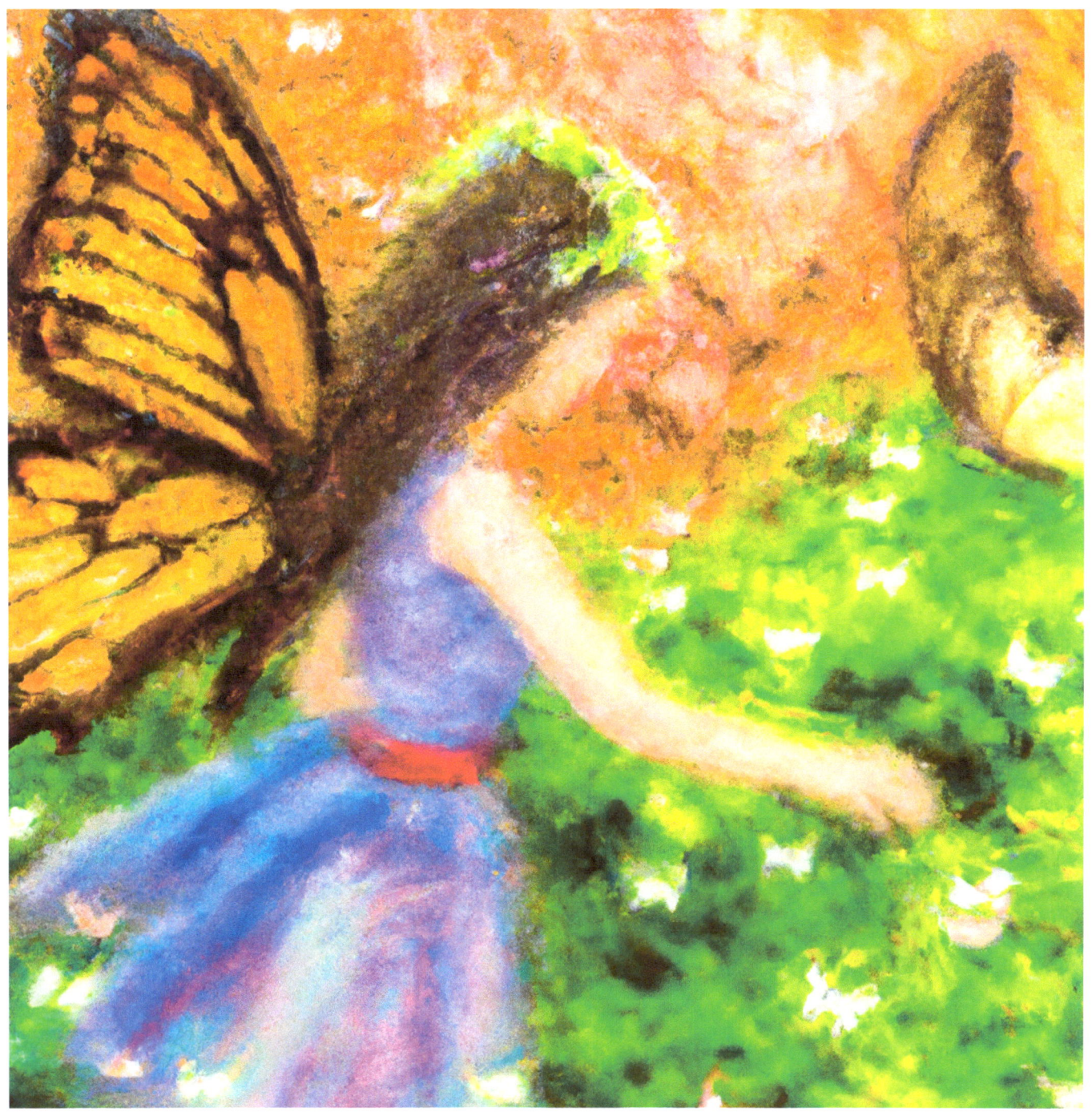

Impressionist Fairy Prints by Julie Ann Shaffer

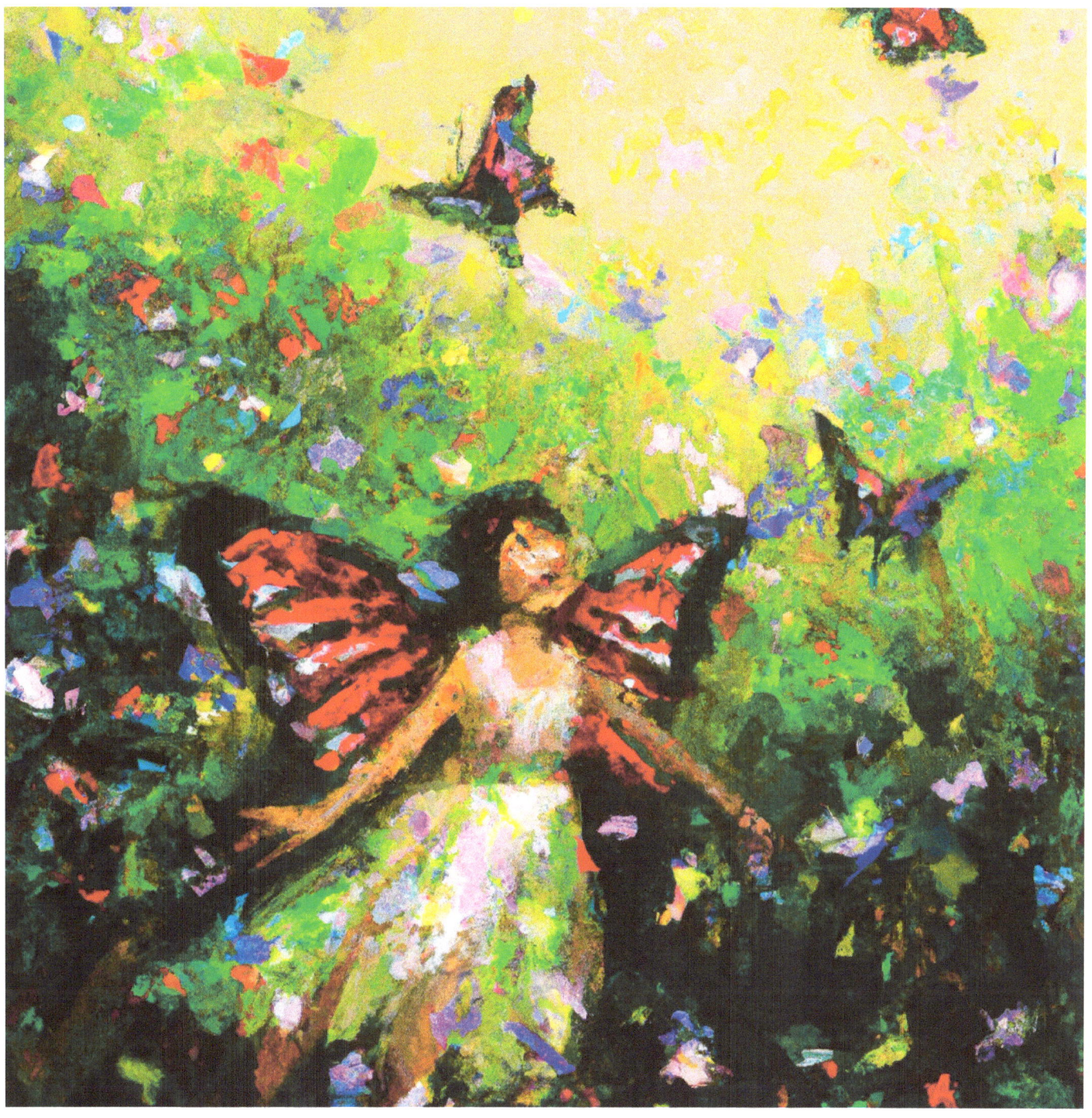

Impressionist Fairy Prints by Julie Ann Shaffer

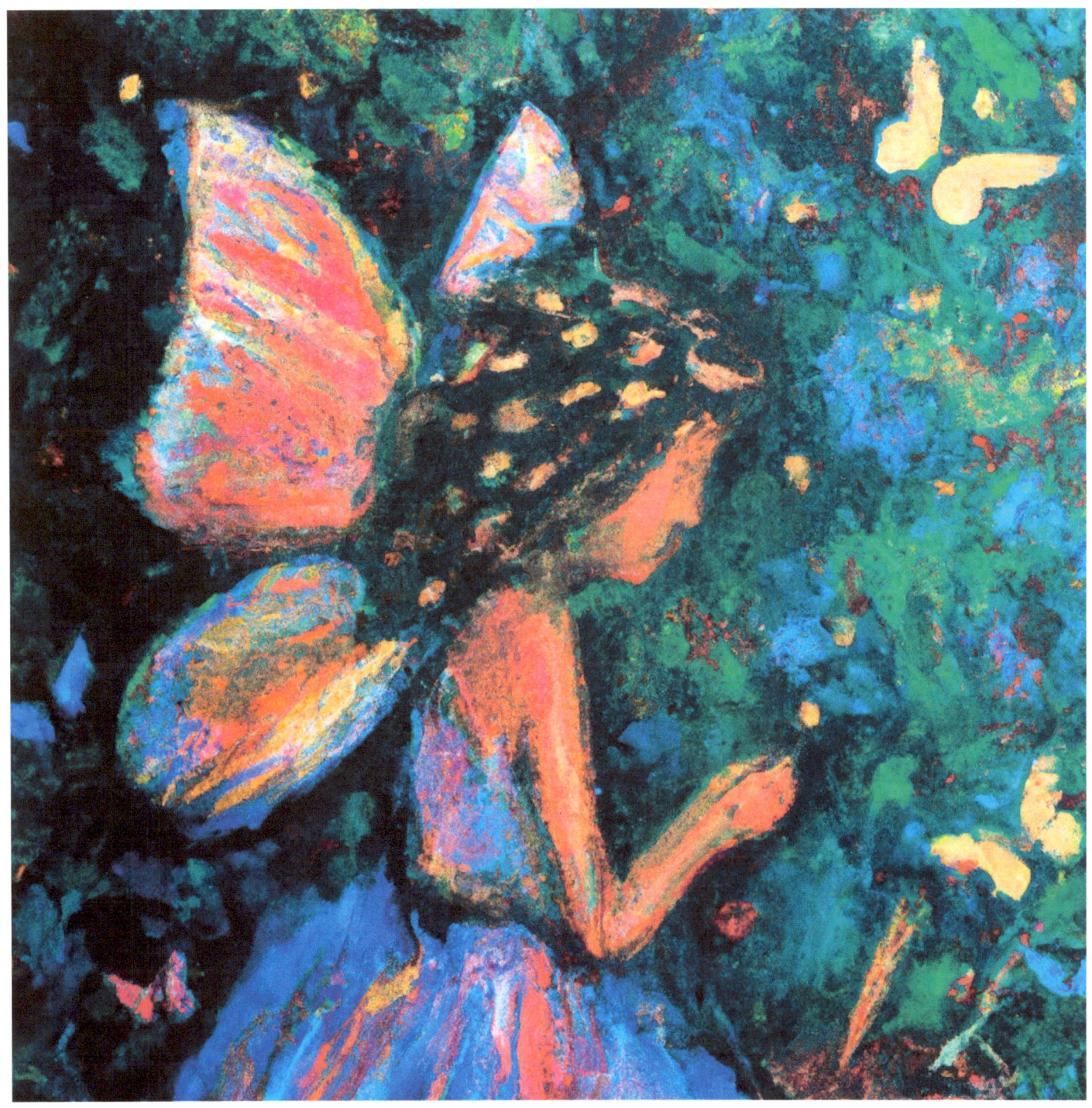

Impressionist Fairy Prints by Julie Ann Shaffer

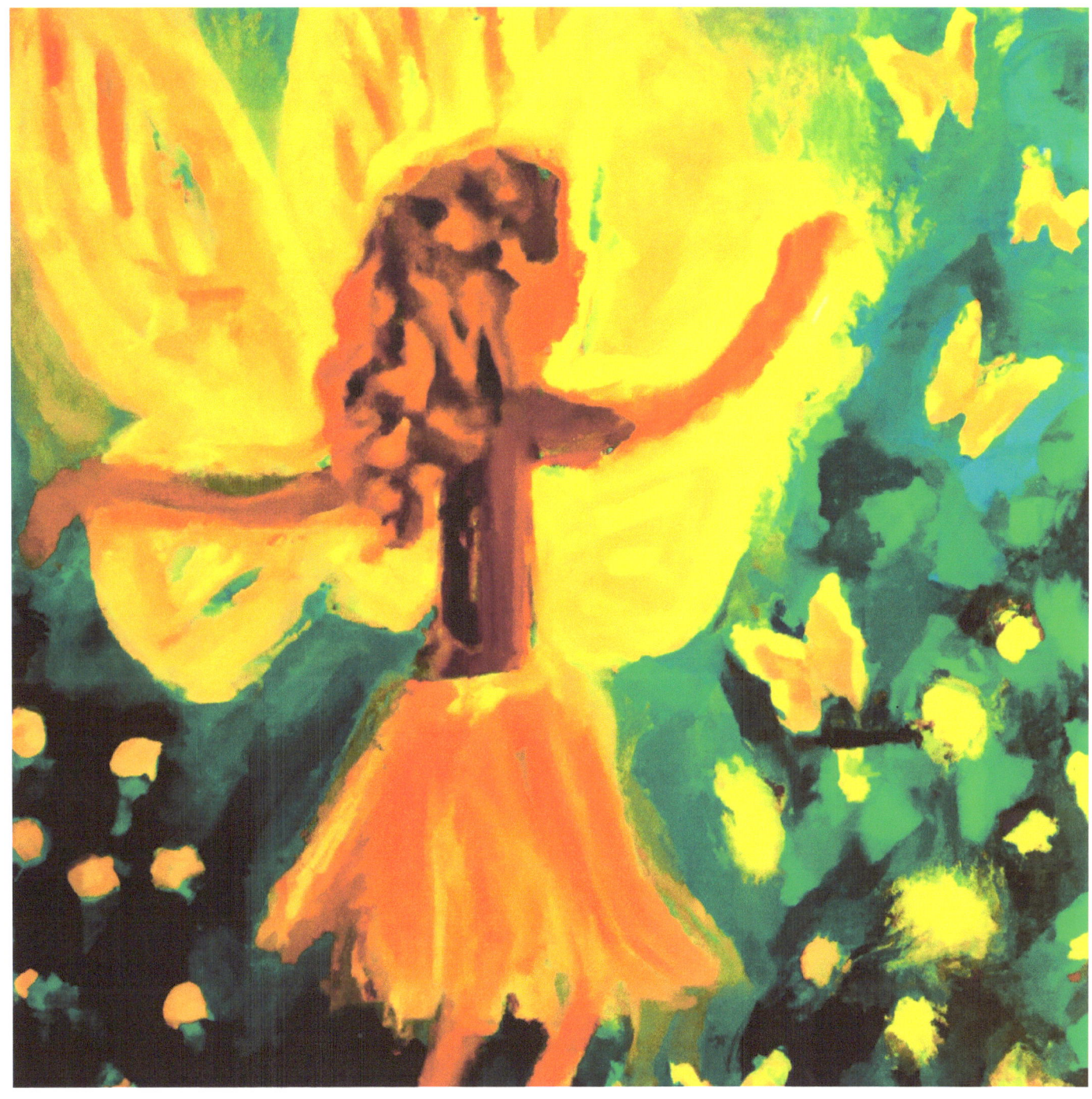

Impressionist Fairy Prints by Julie Ann Shaffer

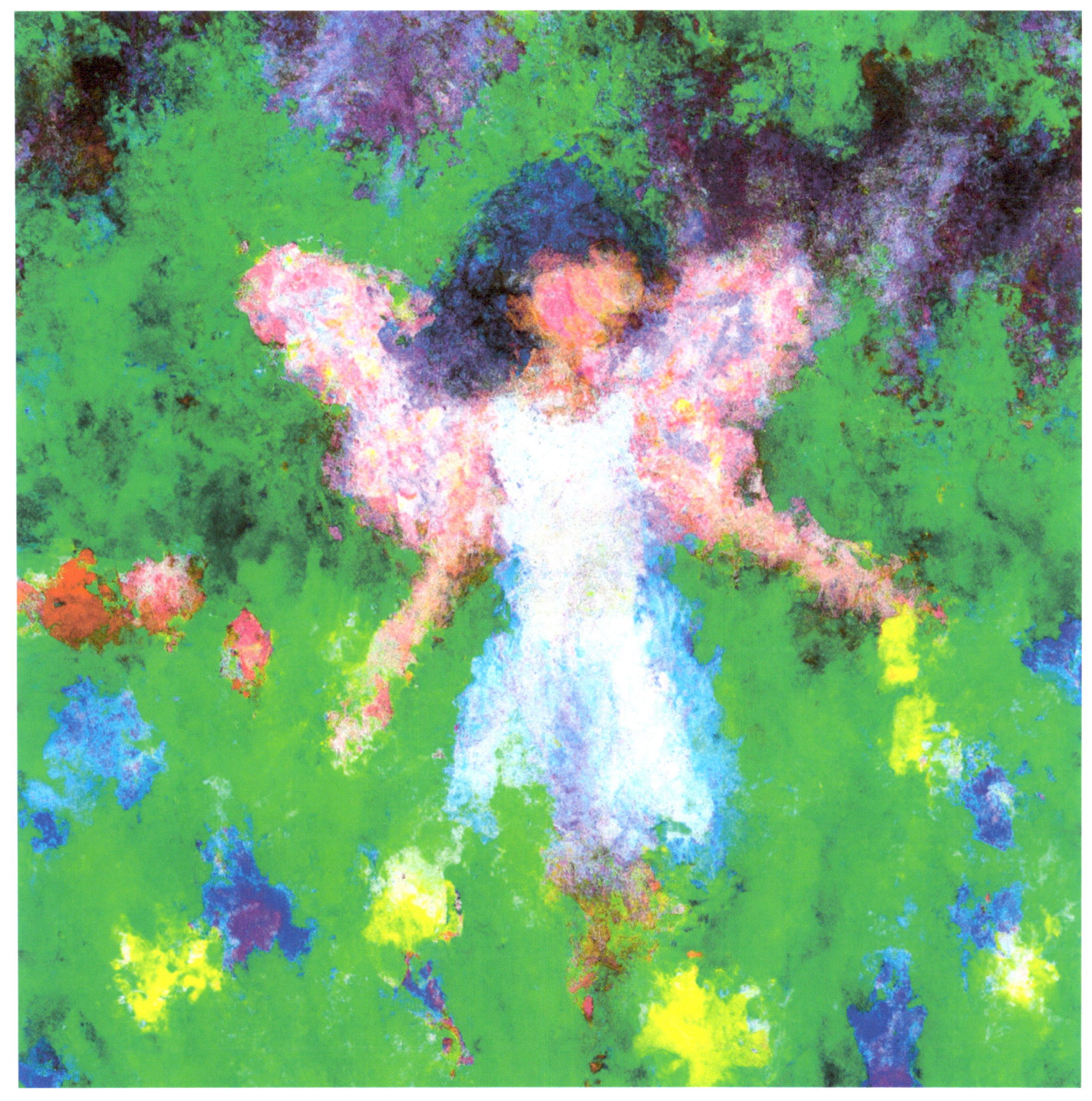

Impressionist Fairy Prints by Julie Ann Shaffer

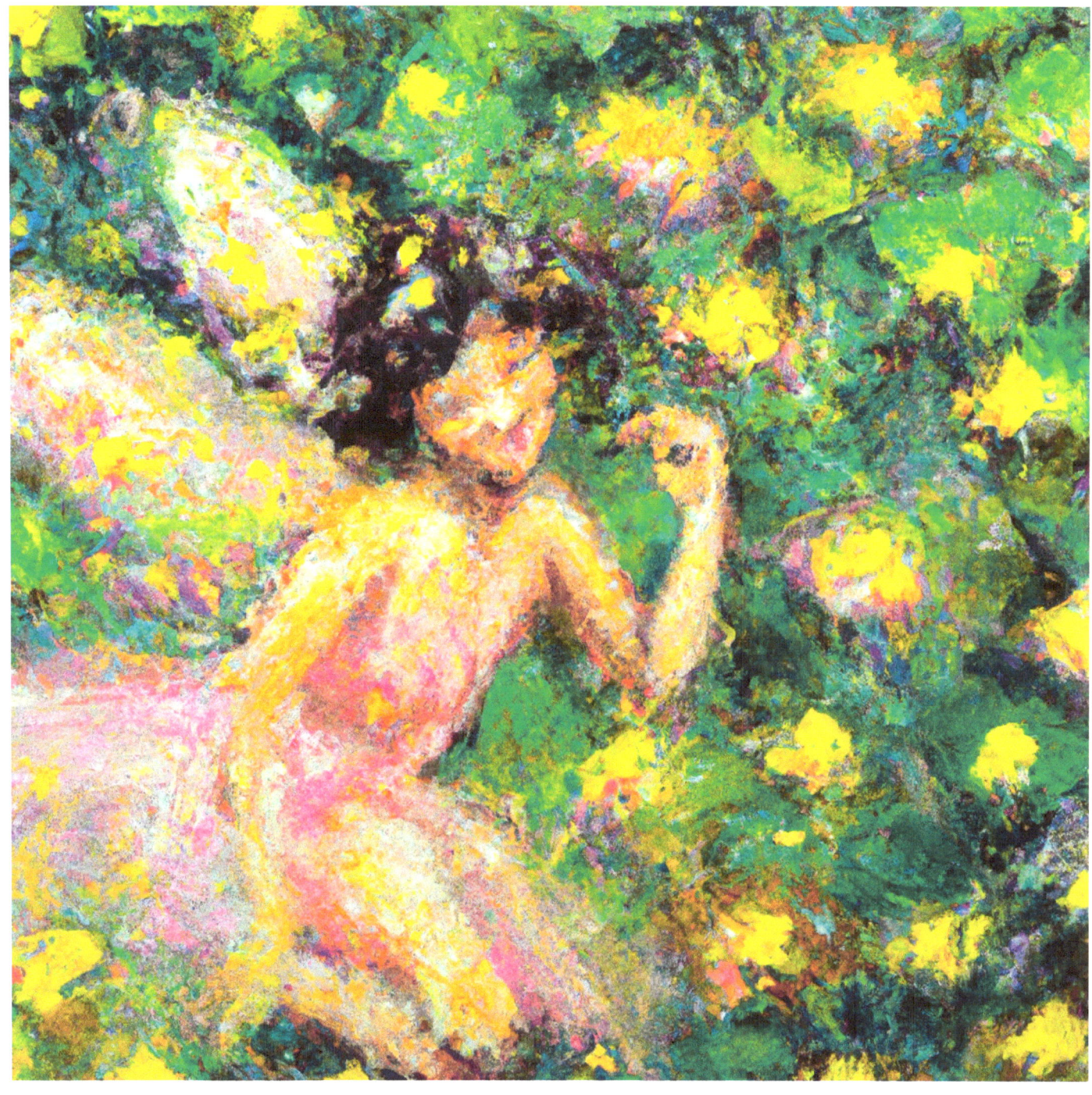

Impressionist Fairy Prints by Julie Ann Shaffer

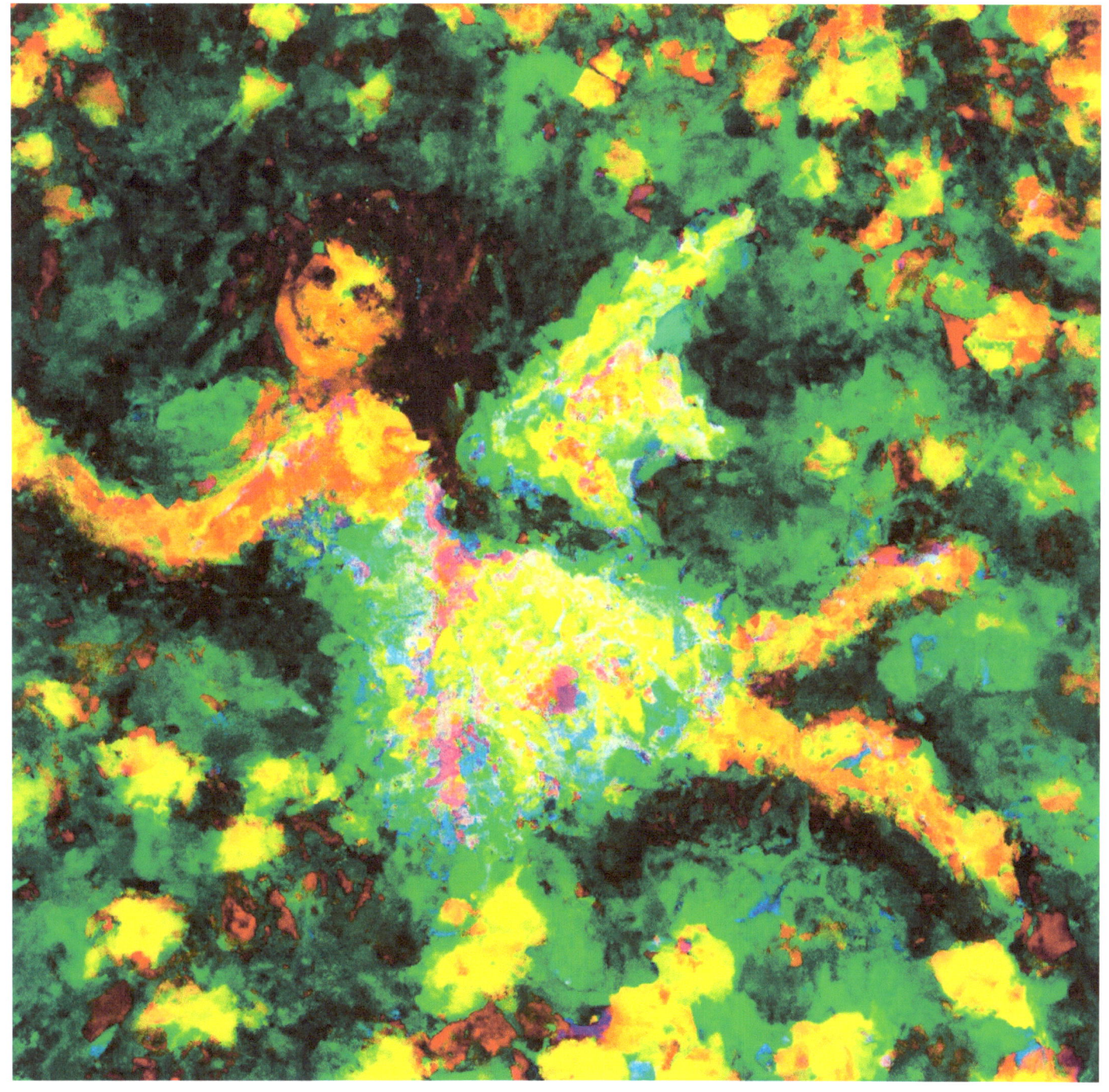

Impressionist Fairy Prints by Julie Ann Shaffer

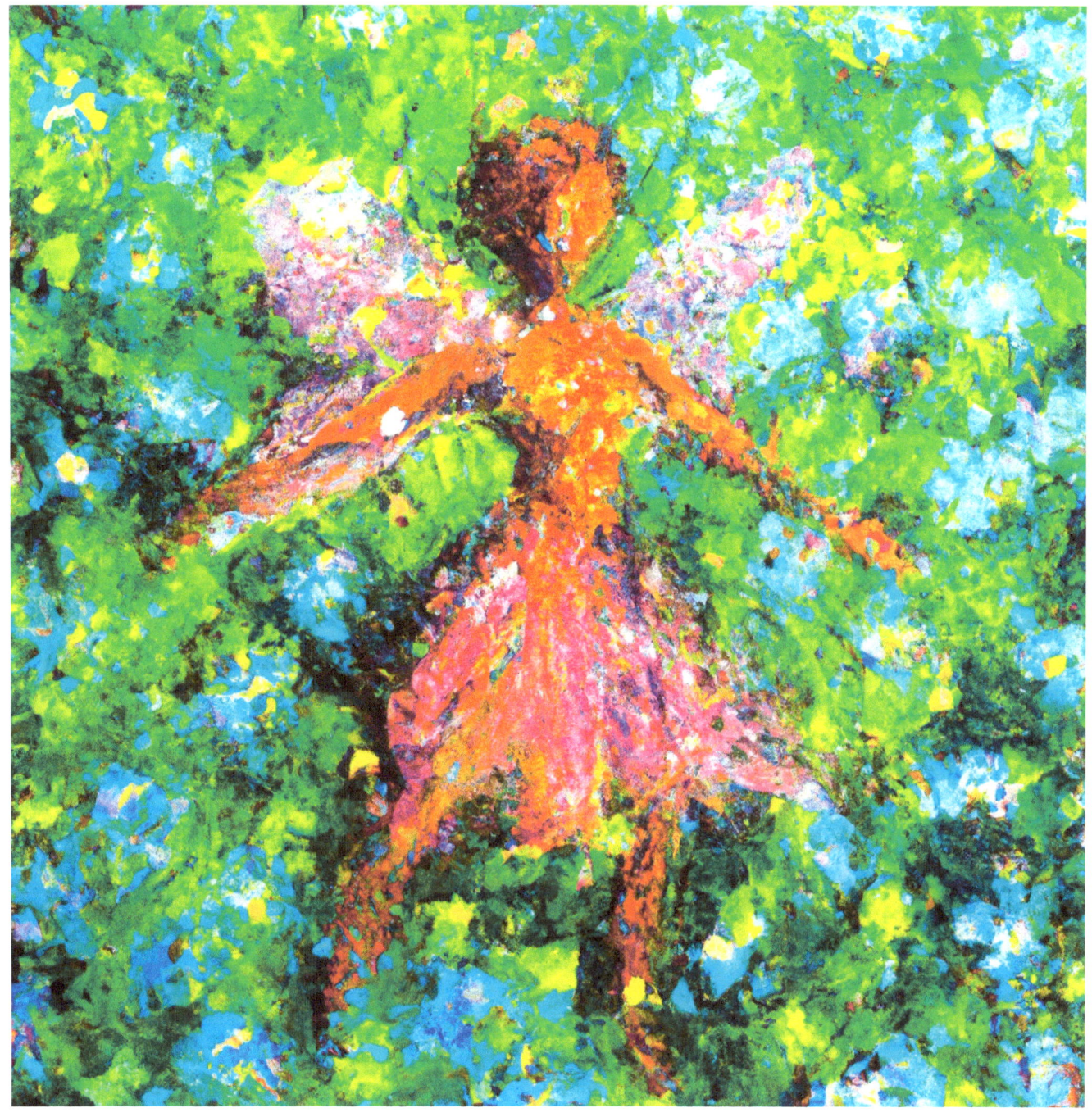

Impressionist Fairy Prints by Julie Ann Shaffer

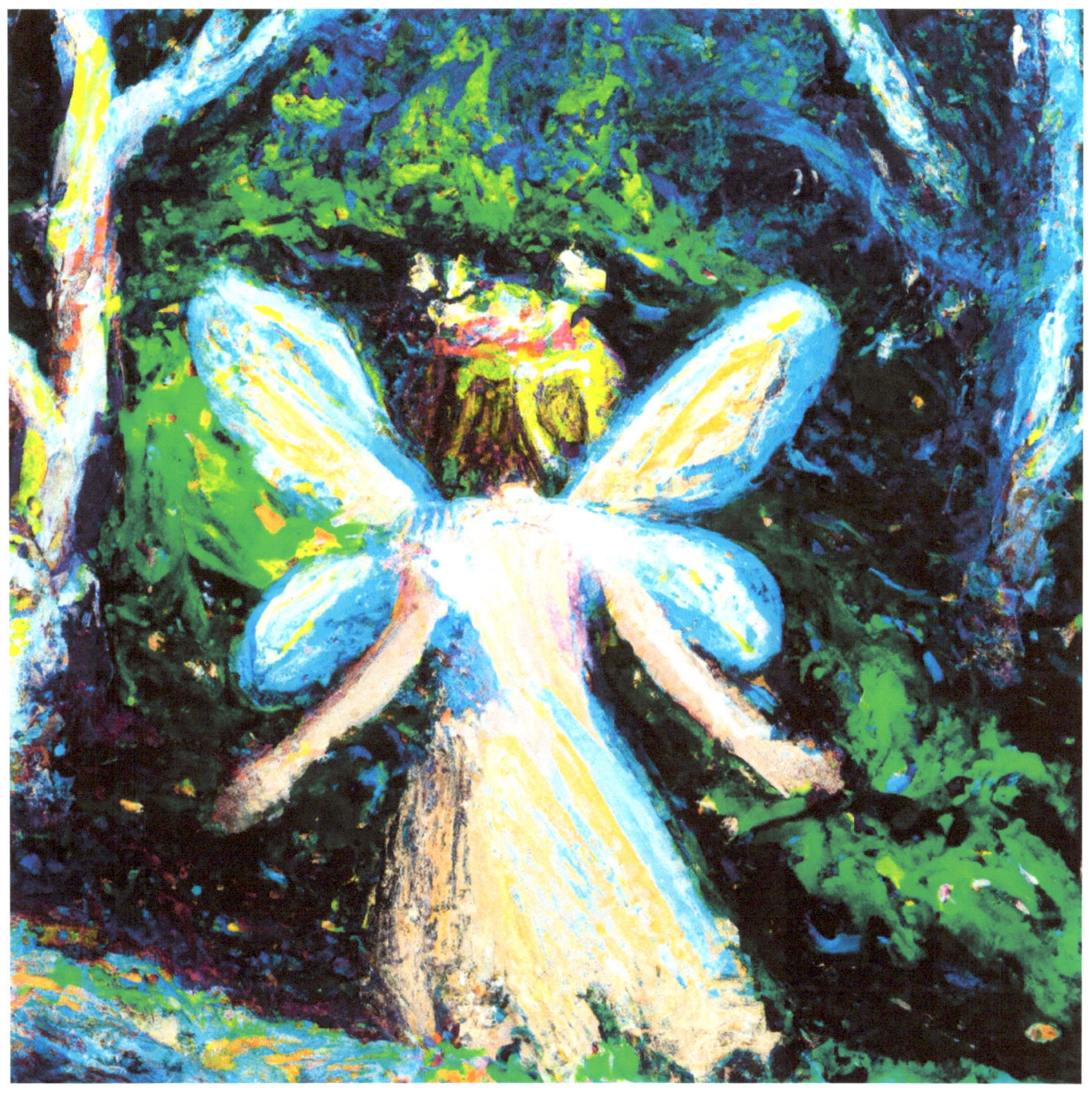

Impressionist Fairy Prints by Julie Ann Shaffer

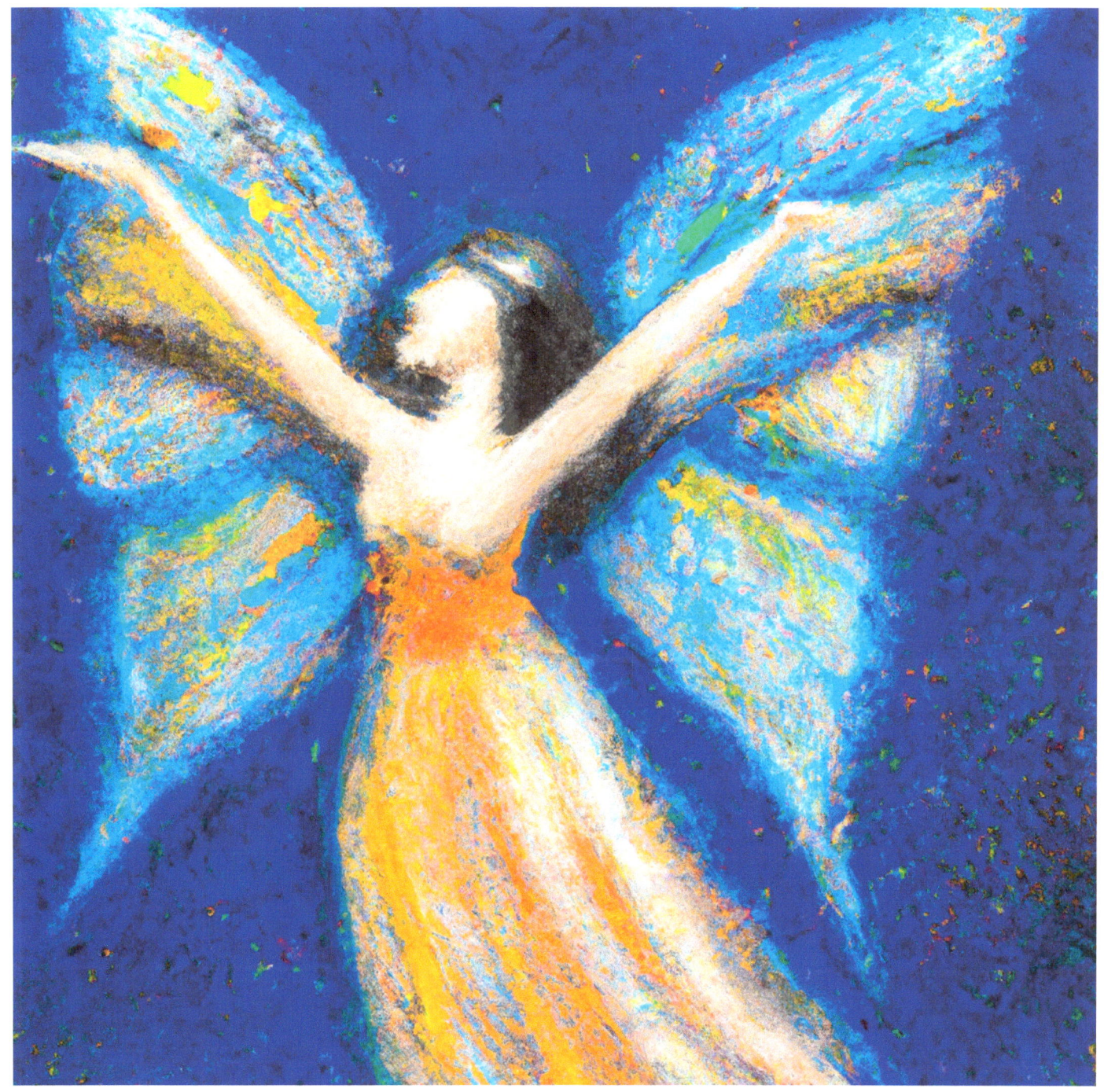

Impressionist Fairy Prints by Julie Ann Shaffer

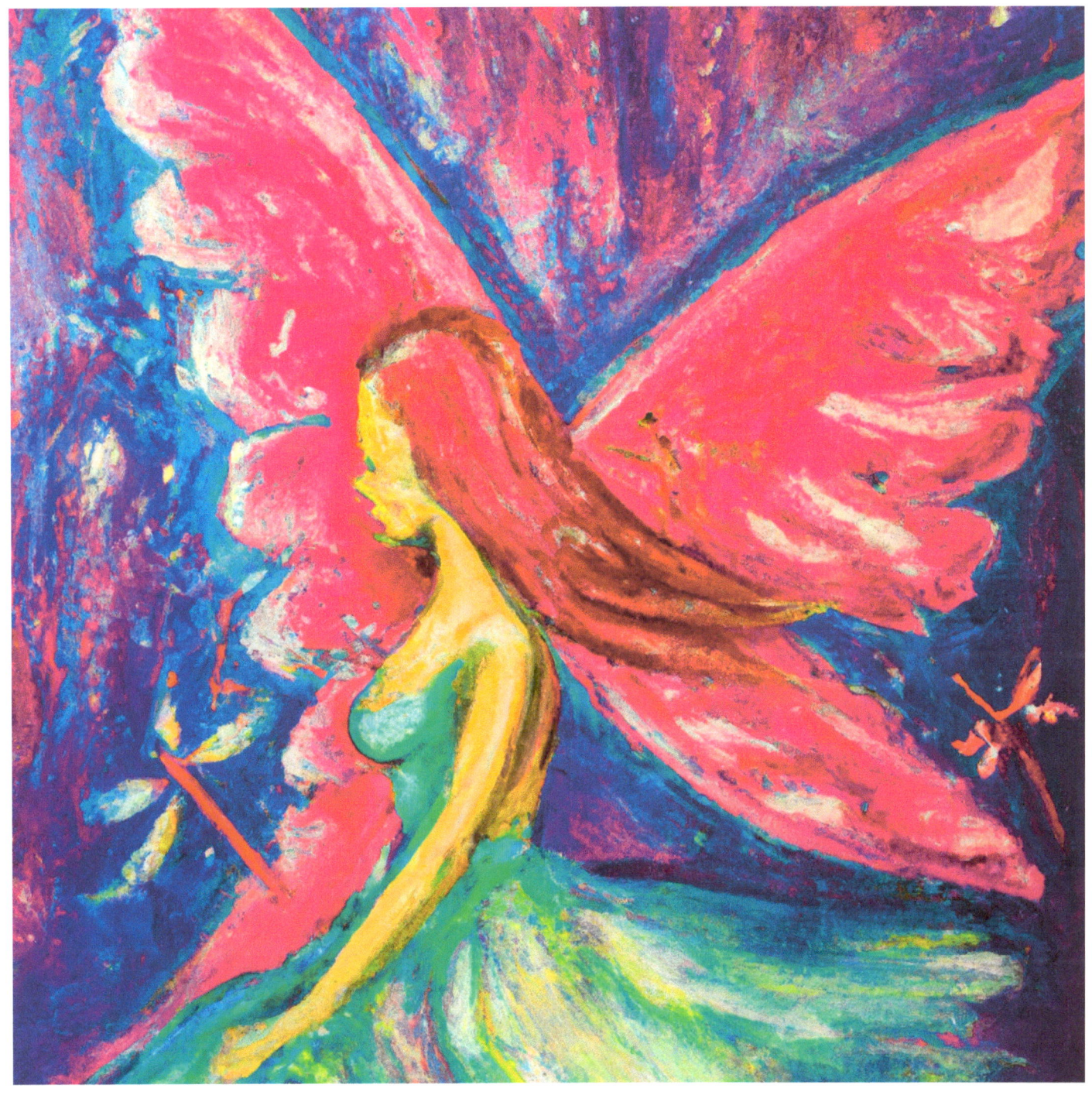

Impressionist Fairy Prints by Julie Ann Shaffer

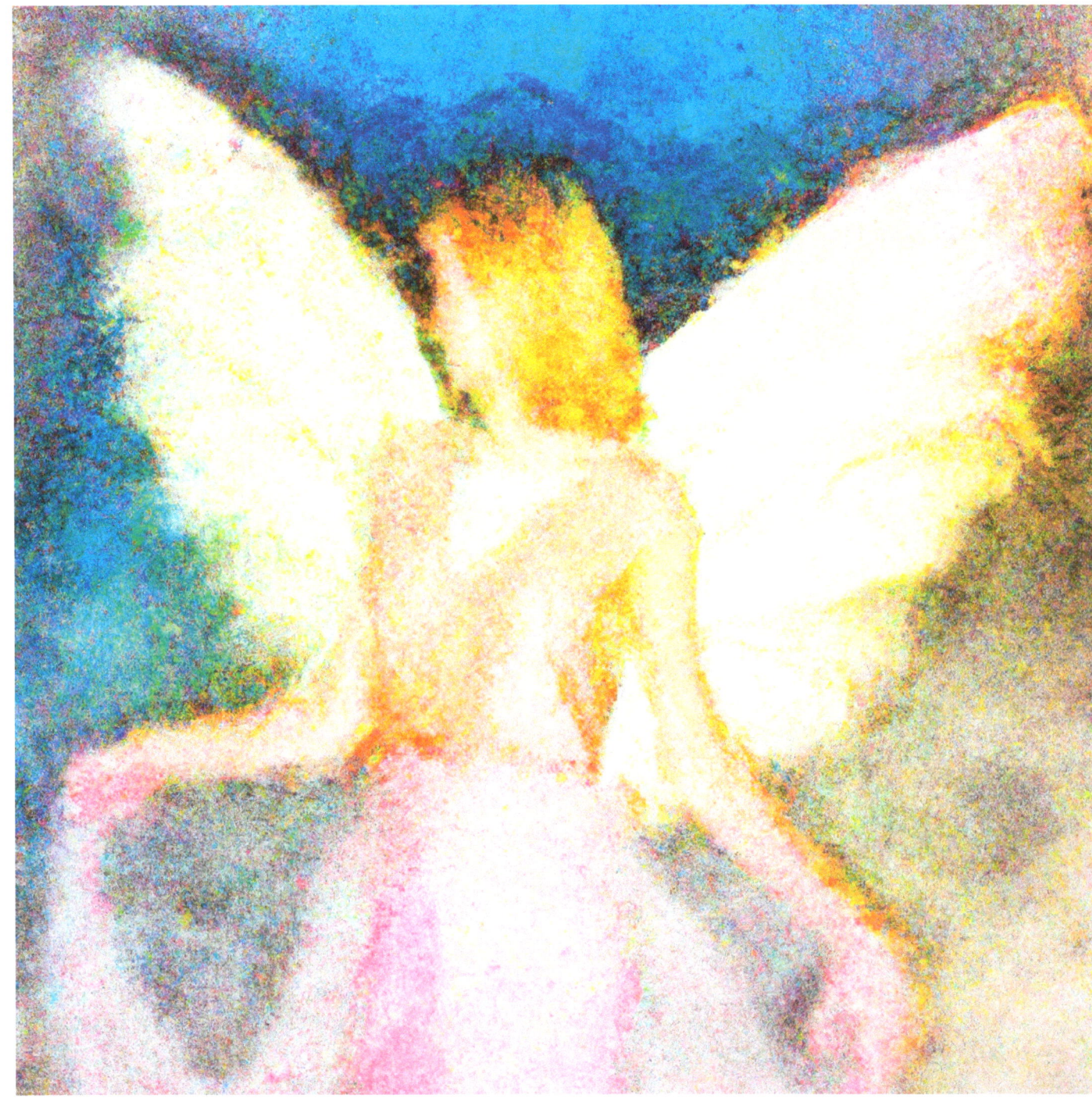

Impressionist Fairy Prints by Julie Ann Shaffer

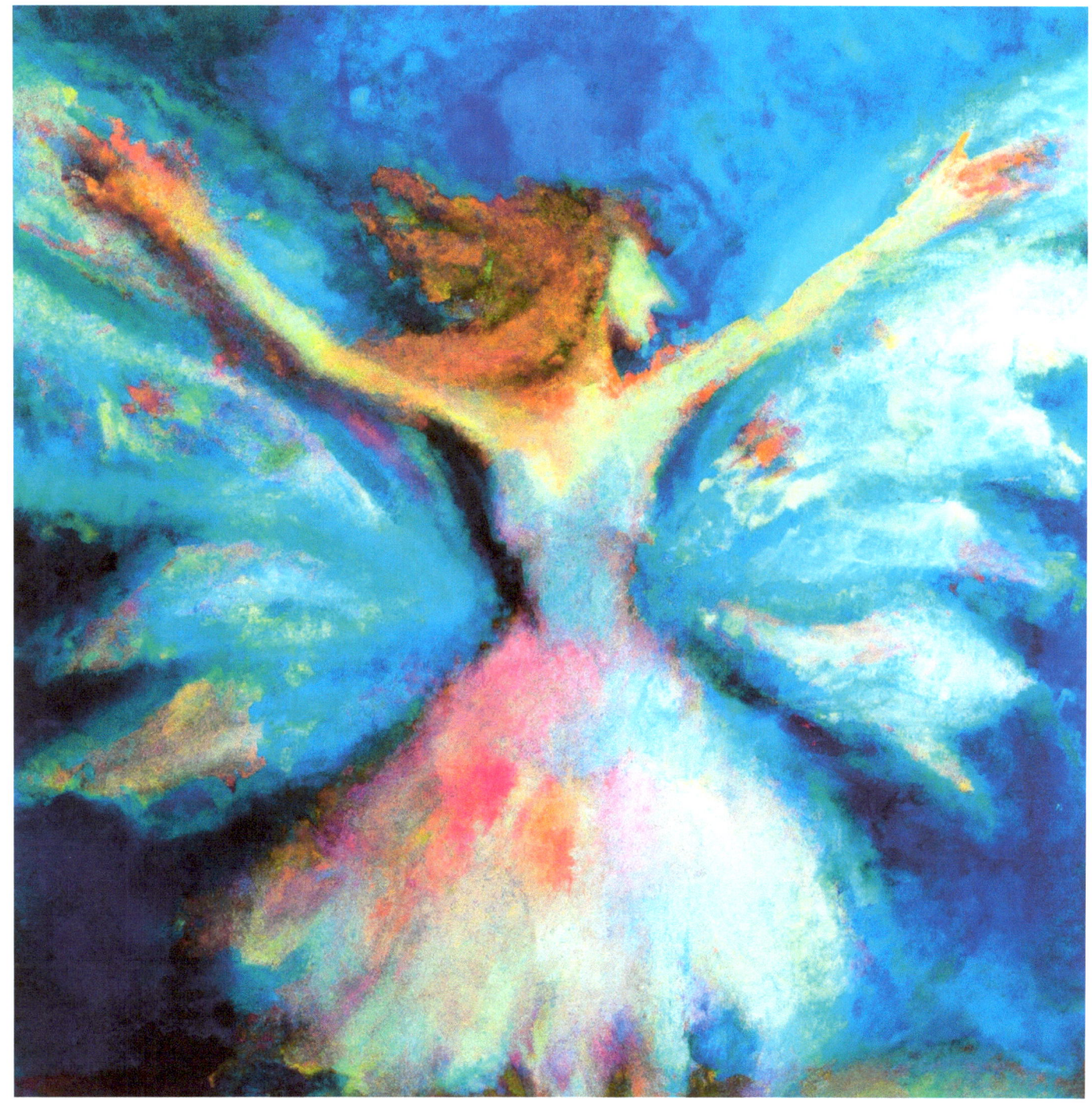

Impressionist Fairy Prints by Julie Ann Shaffer

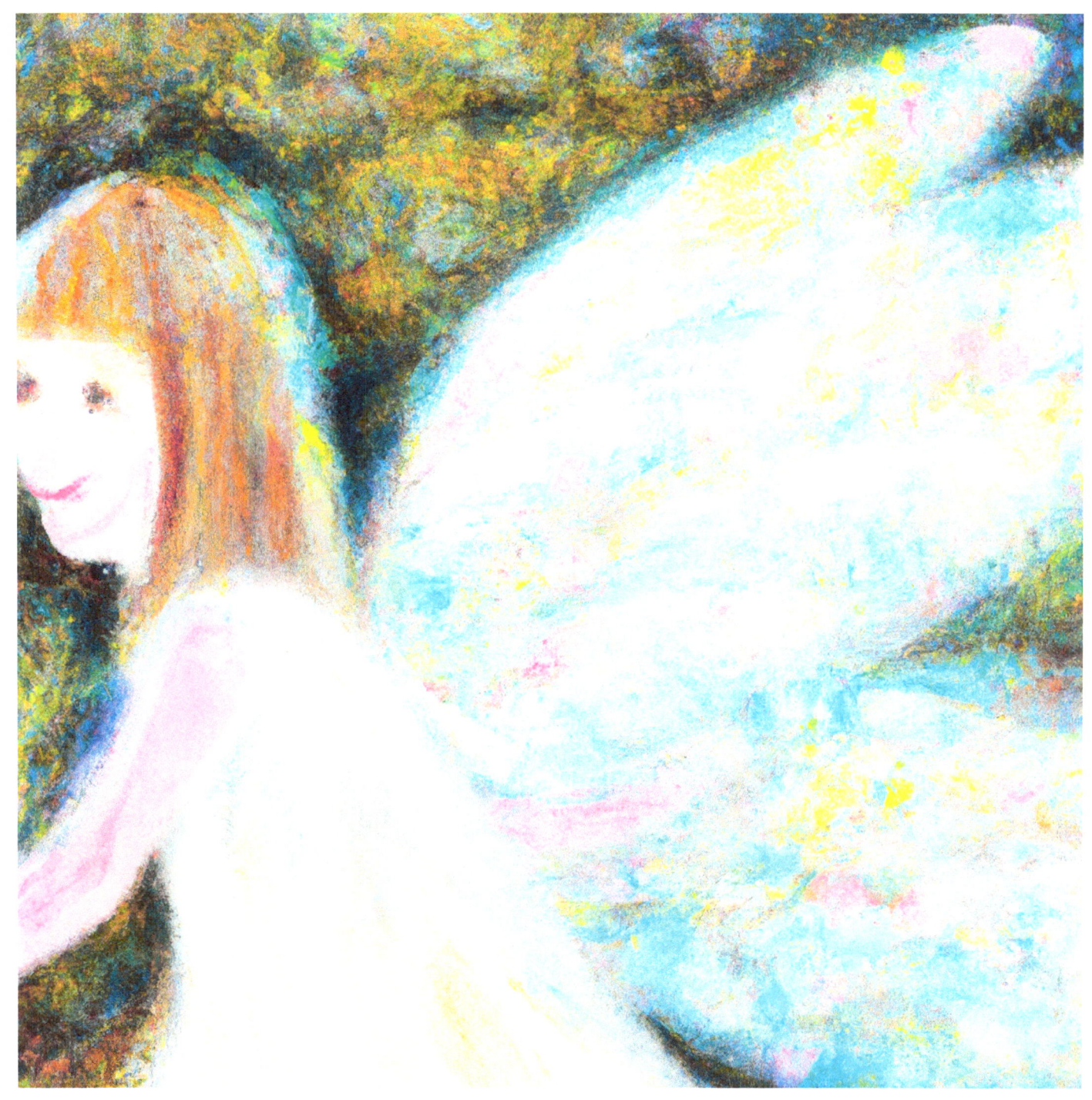

Impressionist Fairy Prints by Julie Ann Shaffer

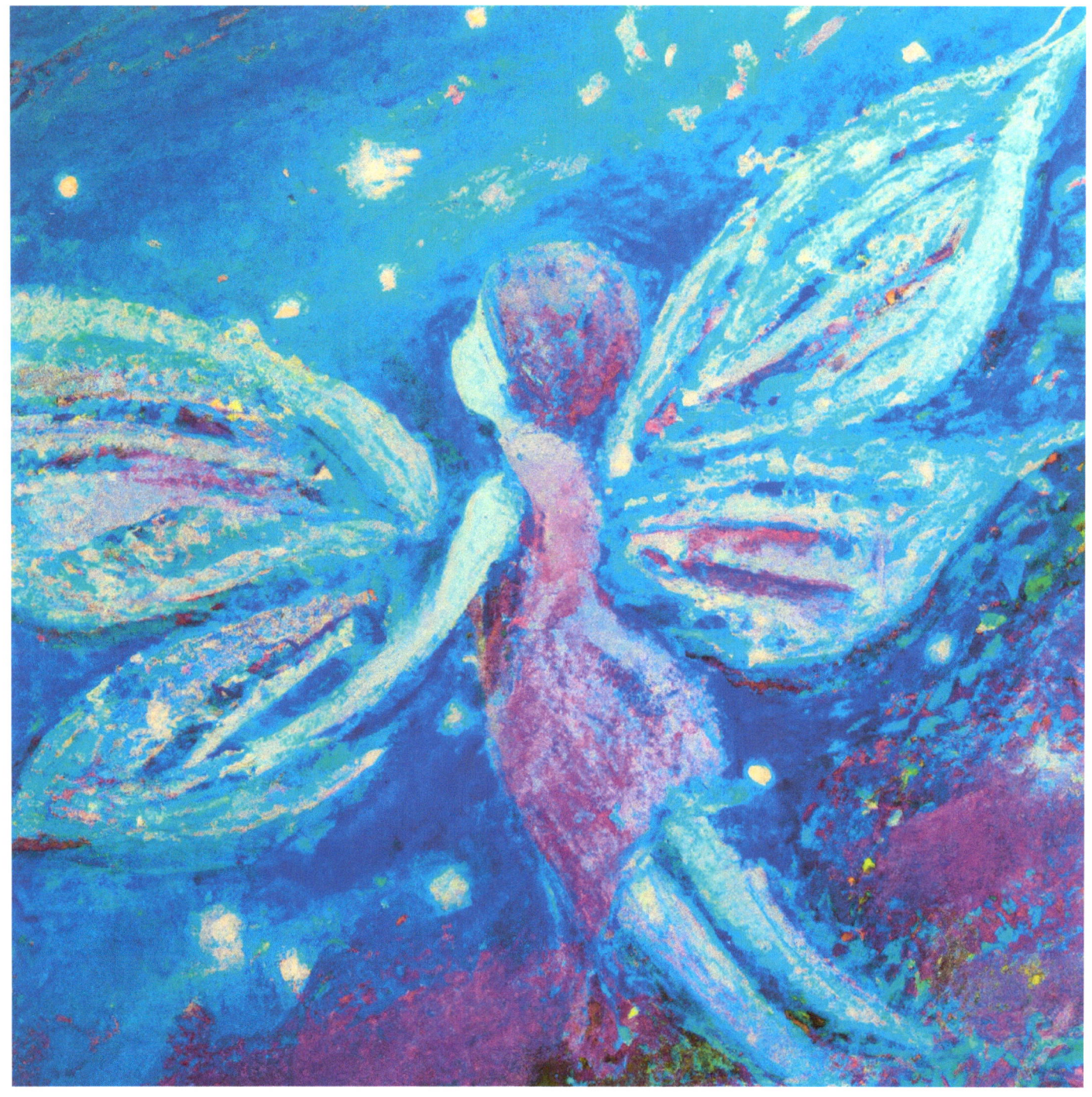

Impressionist Fairy Prints by Julie Ann Shaffer

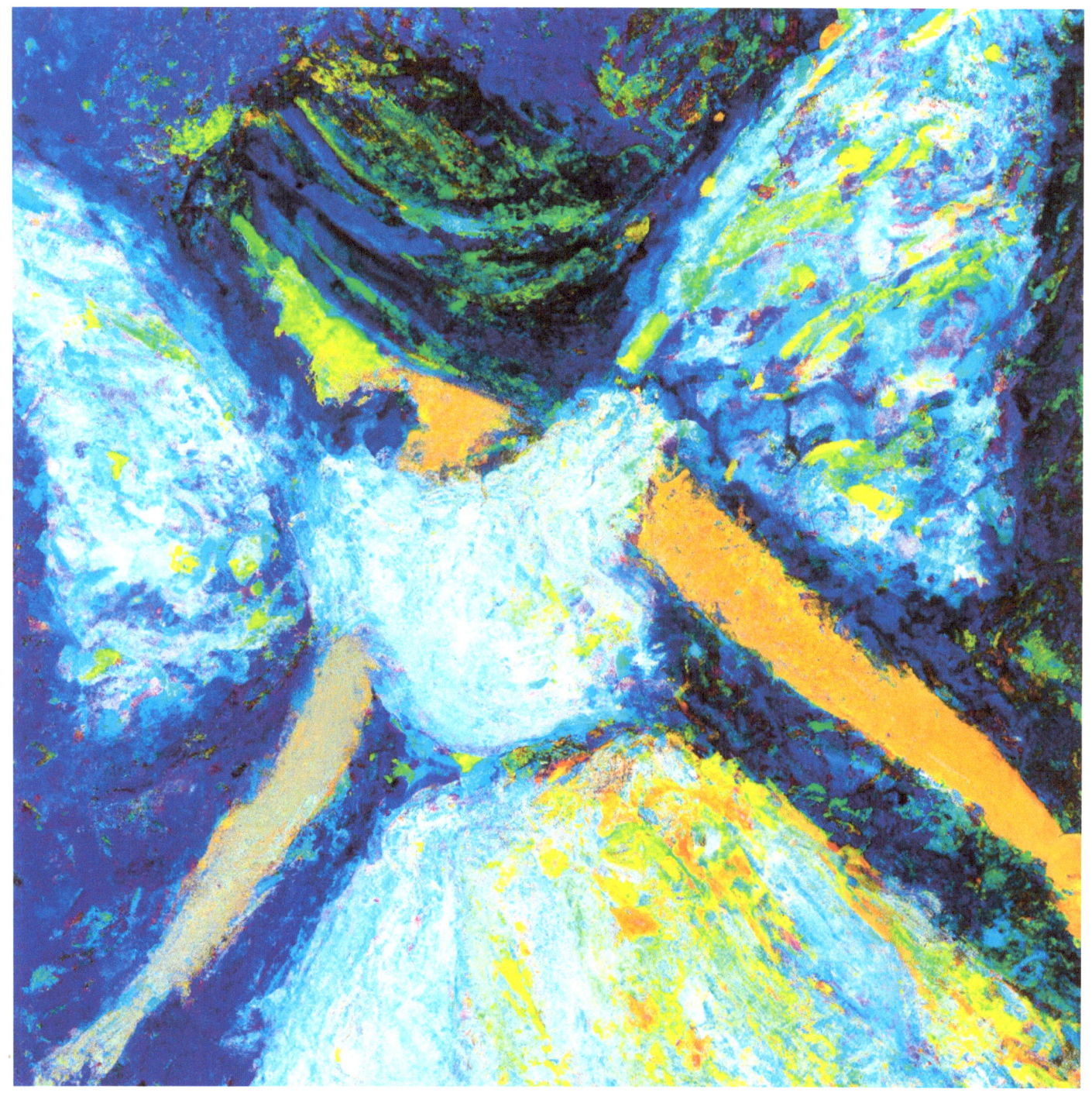

Impressionist Fairy Prints by Julie Ann Shaffer

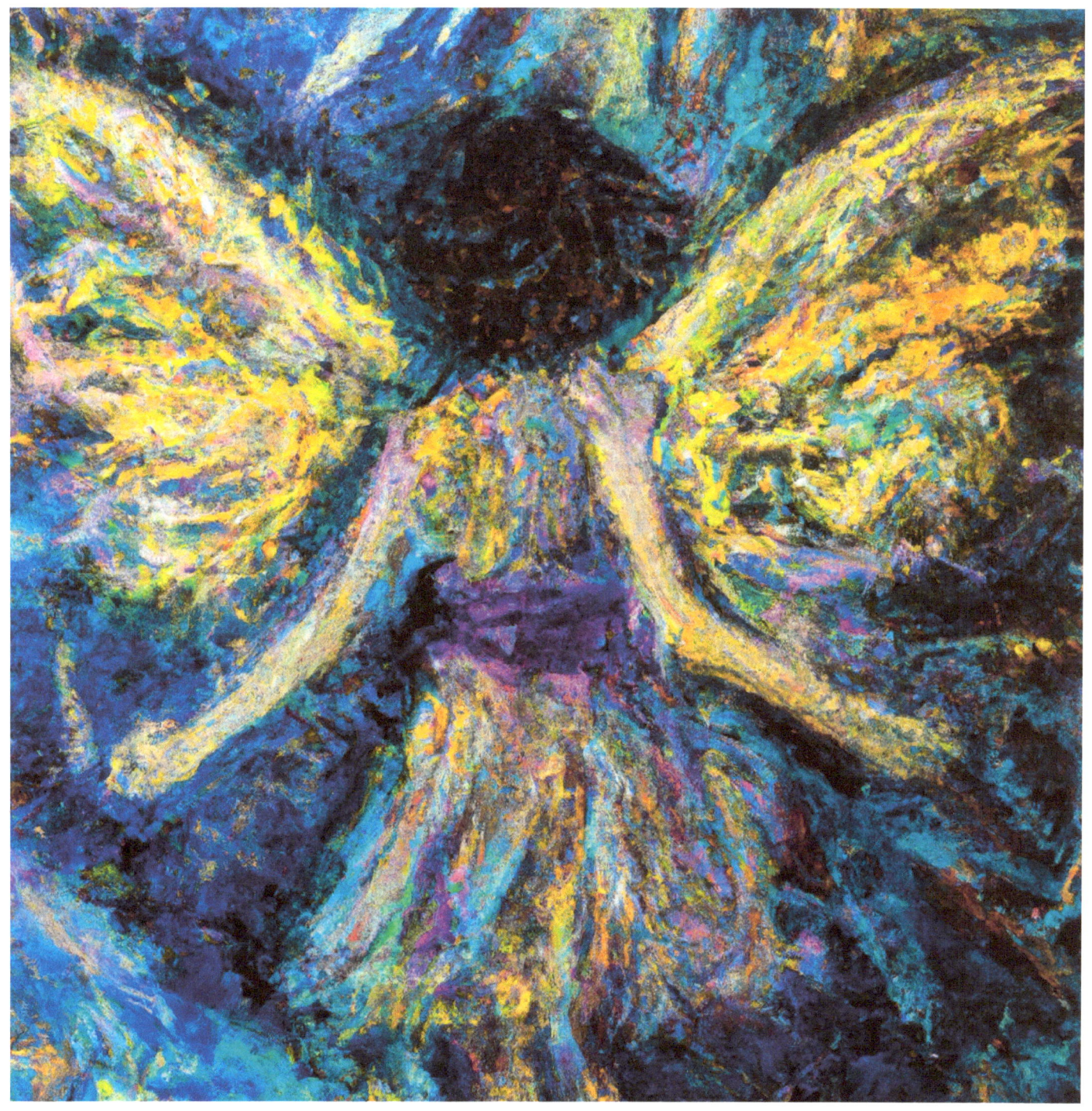

Impressionist Fairy Prints by Julie Ann Shaffer

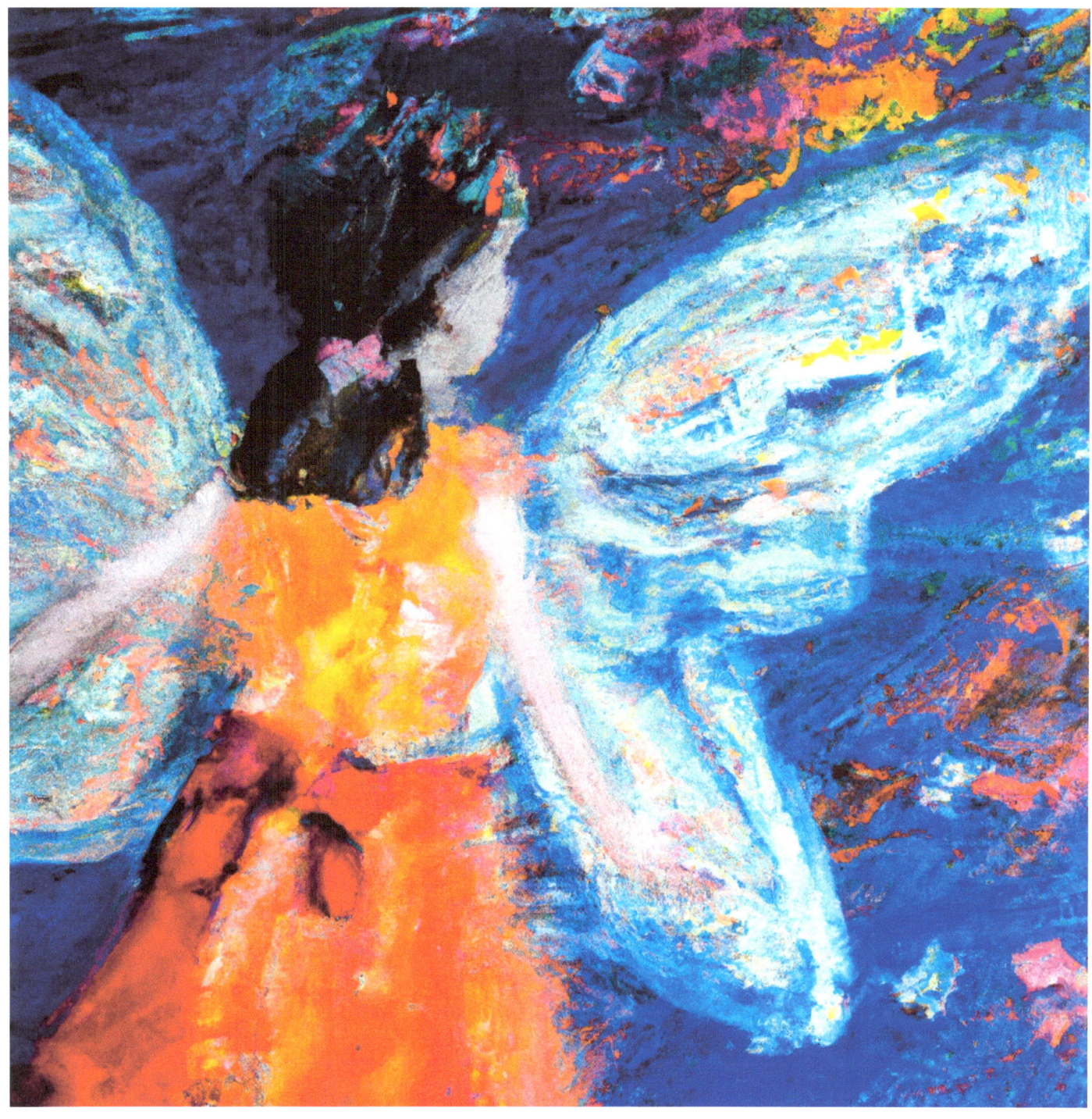

Impressionist Fairy Prints by Julie Ann Shaffer

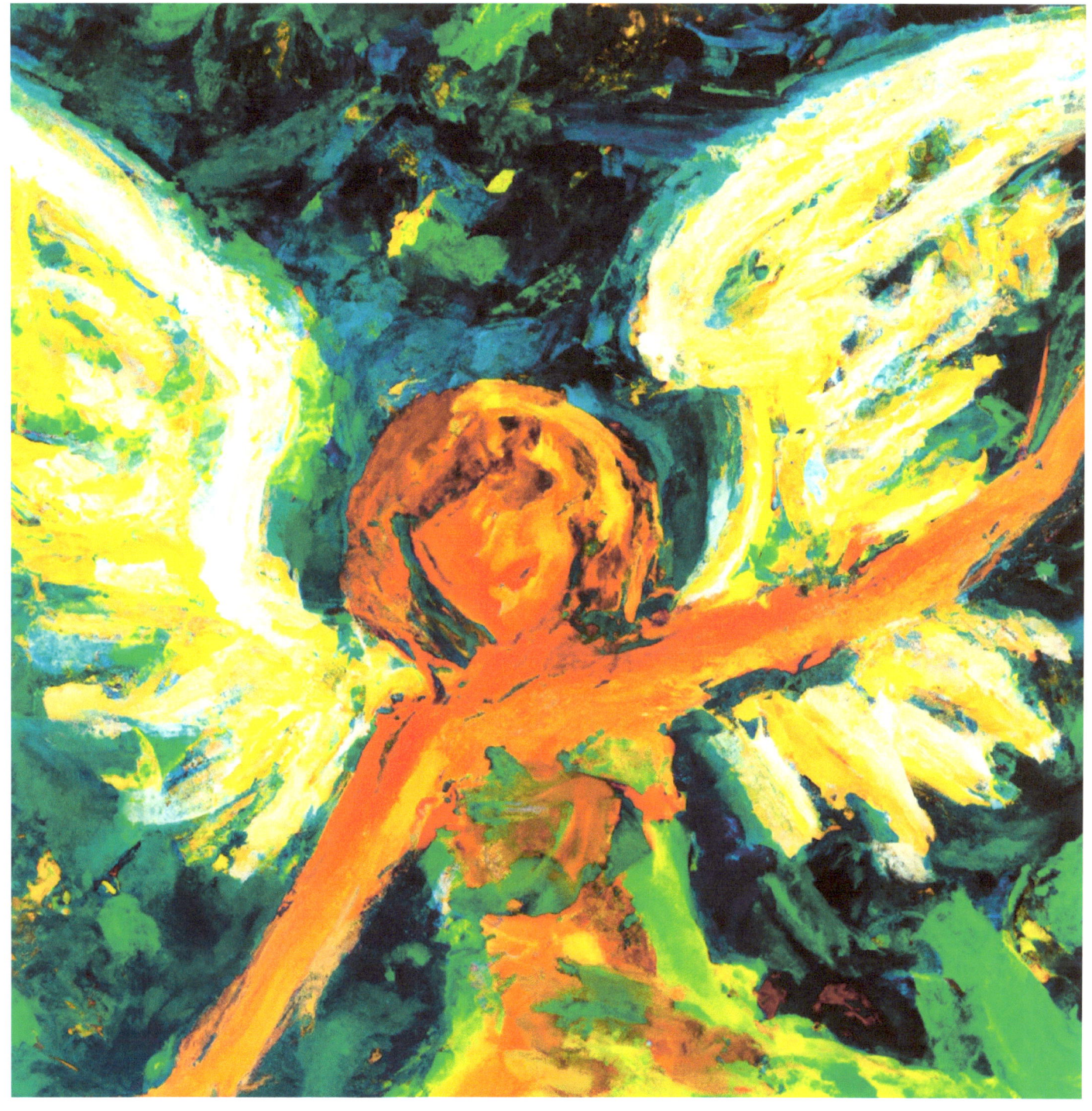

Impressionist Fairy Prints by Julie Ann Shaffer

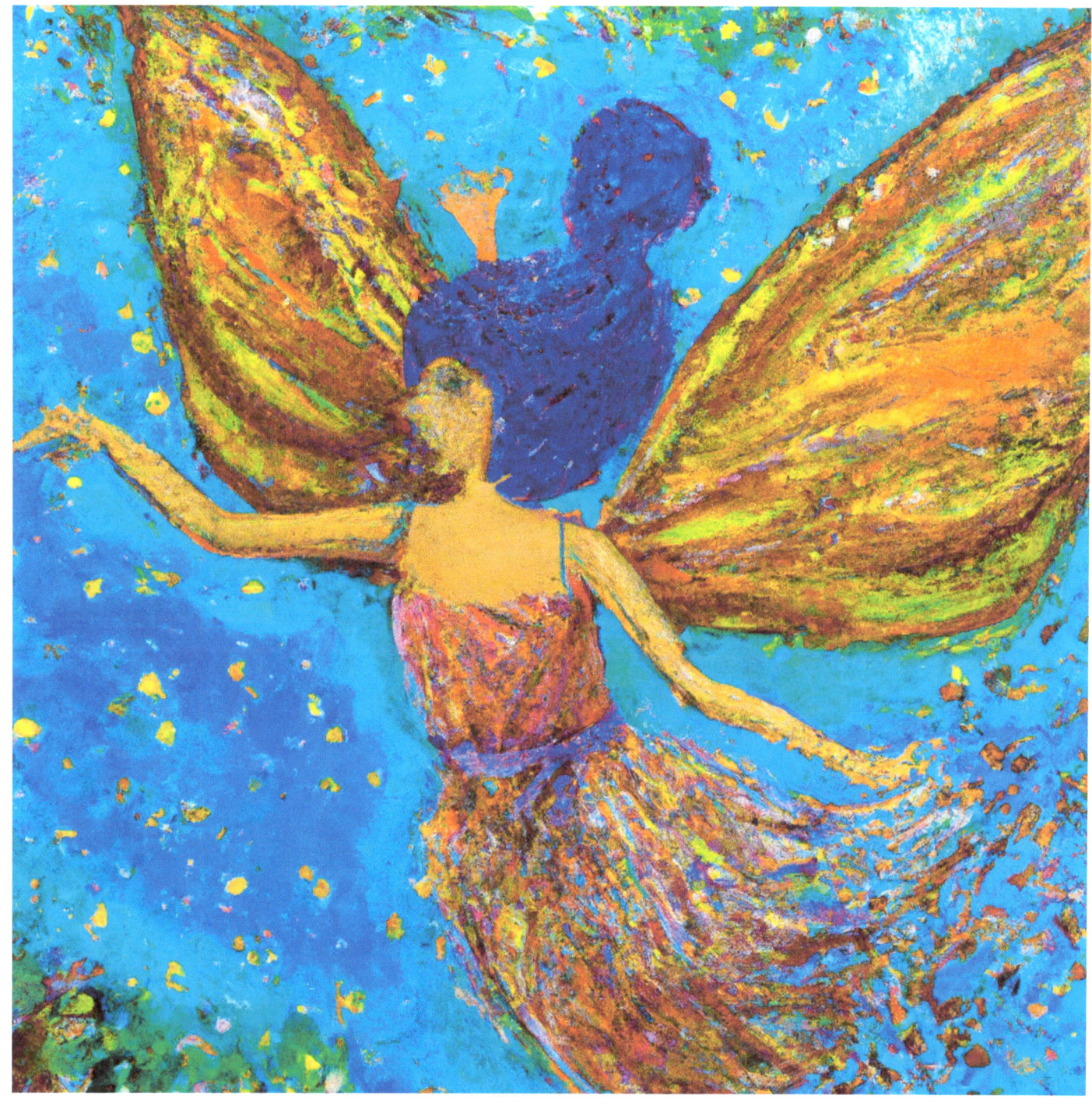

Impressionist Fairy Prints by Julie Ann Shaffer